HOW TO BUDGET AND SAVE MONEY FOR BEGINNERS

Transform Your Finances, Automate Your Money, and Live a Rich Life with This Proven System for Financial Success

Jerry R. Schaefer

i

OTHER BOOKS BY SAME AUTHOR

1. THE PATH TO LONG-TERM INVESTMENT
2. FINANCIAL INDEPENDENCE WITH 70% SAVING
3. ONE YEAR TO FINANCIAL FREEDOM
4. INVESTING STRATEGIES FOR ANY BUDGET
5. FROM YOUR FIRST $100K
6. HOW TO INVEST FOR BEGINNERS

TABLE OF CONTENTS

INTRODUCTION

In the hustle and bustle of daily life, the idea of establishing a paycheck routine might seem like just another financial management strategy. However, delving deeper reveals that a well-crafted paycheck routine is not just a method; it's a powerful tool that can shape your financial destiny and lead you on the path to true financial freedom.

At its core, a paycheck routine is about creating a systematic approach to managing your money. It transforms the chaotic dance of income and expenses into a structured rhythm that aligns with your financial goals. The power lies in its simplicity and consistency – two elements often overlooked in the world of personal finance.

Firstly, simplicity is the cornerstone of an effective paycheck routine. Many individuals find themselves overwhelmed by the complexities of budgeting, investing, and saving. A paycheck routine simplifies this process by streamlining your financial actions. It's not about juggling multiple accounts or deciphering intricate investment strategies; it's about creating a straightforward plan that anyone can follow.

Imagine your finances as a puzzle, and a paycheck routine as the frame that holds all the pieces together. It eliminates the need for constant decision-making, reducing the mental load associated with managing money. Instead of navigating a maze of financial choices, you're guided by a clear and uncomplicated path.

The second key element is consistency. In the realm of personal finance, consistency is more than a virtue – it's a game-changer. A well-established paycheck routine ensures that your financial actions are not sporadic but rather a steady, reliable stream. This consistency is crucial for building financial habits that stand the test of time.

Consider it as developing a habit as routine as brushing your teeth. When your paycheck routine becomes second nature, financial decisions no longer feel like a burden. Just as you automatically reach for your toothbrush in the morning, your financial actions become ingrained, leading to a more sustainable and stress-free financial life.

The power of a paycheck routine is particularly evident in the concept of paying yourself first. Instead of letting money slip through your fingers with impulsive spending, a paycheck routine prioritizes your financial goals. This means allocating a portion of your income to savings and investments before anything else.

Paying yourself first might seem counterintuitive in a world where bills and expenses demand immediate attention. However, this shift in perspective is what makes a paycheck routine transformative. It instills the habit of intentional saving, laying the groundwork for future financial success. It's not about what's left at the end of the month; it's about deliberately setting aside funds for your dreams and aspirations.

Moreover, a paycheck routine offers a shield against the often unpredictable nature of life. Unexpected expenses, emergencies, or market fluctuations lose their power to derail your financial stability when you have a structured routine in place. By automating your money flow, you create a buffer that safeguards you from the financial turbulence that might otherwise send shockwaves through your life.

In essence, understanding the power of a paycheck routine is about recognizing that financial success is not about complex strategies or getting lucky in the market. It's about embracing simplicity, cultivating consistency, and prioritizing your financial well-being. A paycheck routine is not just a plan; it's a mindset shift that empowers you to take control of your money, making the journey to financial freedom not only achievable but sustainable.

Chapter 2: Step One - Automate Your Money Flow

2.1 Why Automate?

In the journey toward financial freedom, the power of automation emerges as a guiding force in shaping a secure and stress-free financial future. Step One of our three-step paycheck routine revolves around the fundamental question: Why automate? Understanding the profound impact of automation is the key to unlocking the doors to financial well-being.

At its essence, automation brings a level of efficiency and consistency to your financial life that manual management often struggles to achieve. The old adage "out of sight, out of mind" takes on a new meaning as you embark on the journey of automating your money flow. By automating financial processes, you remove the burden of constant decision-making and reduce the risk of succumbing to impulsive spending.

One of the primary advantages of automation is the elimination of procrastination. How many times have we promised ourselves to set aside money for savings or investments, only to find that life's distractions lead us astray? Automation acts as a reliable guardian, ensuring that your financial commitments are met without the need for continual reminders or self-discipline.

Imagine your paycheck landing in your account, and without lifting a finger, a predetermined portion is whisked away to your savings account and another to your 401k. This seamless transfer happens automatically, allowing you to focus on the more enjoyable aspects of life rather than constantly worrying about managing your money.

Moreover, automation introduces a level of consistency that is crucial for building lasting financial habits. The erratic nature of manually moving money can lead to inconsistencies in savings and investments. With automation, a sense of routine is established – a routine that prioritizes paying yourself first and actively contributes to the growth of your financial reserves.

But why is paying yourself first so pivotal? It's about recognizing your financial goals as a priority rather than an afterthought. Automating this process ensures that your savings and investments receive the attention they deserve right from the moment your paycheck lands in your account. It's a proactive approach that sets the stage for financial success.

Another compelling aspect of automation is its ability to create a financial safety net. Life is unpredictable, and emergencies or unexpected expenses can throw even the most meticulous budget into disarray. Automation acts as a protective barrier by diverting a portion of your income into savings, providing a buffer for those unforeseen circumstances. This financial cushion brings peace of mind, knowing that you have a resource to lean on when life takes an unexpected turn.

In the era of technology, embracing automation is not just a choice; it's a smart and strategic move. Various financial platforms and apps make setting up automated transfers a breeze, putting the power to control your financial destiny literally at your fingertips. The convenience and accessibility of these tools ensure that anyone, regardless of financial expertise, can harness the benefits of automation.

In conclusion, the question of "Why automate?" finds its answer in the transformative potential of financial automation. By streamlining your money flow, automation becomes the cornerstone of financial stability and future prosperity. It's not just about making things easier; it's about fundamentally reshaping your relationship with money and setting the stage for a wealthier, more secure tomorrow.

2.2 Setting Up Automatic Transfers

With the decision to automate your money flow comes the pivotal task of setting up automatic transfers – the gears that drive the engine of financial efficiency. In this crucial step of our three-step paycheck routine, we delve into the practical aspect of making automation a reality. It's not just about the why; it's about the how, and setting up automatic transfers is where the rubber meets the road on your journey to financial freedom.

To embark on this process, begin by understanding the anatomy of your paycheck. Your paycheck is not just a number; it's a resource that can be strategically allocated to serve your financial goals. By setting up automatic transfers, you ensure that this resource is directed with precision, each dollar finding its purpose in contributing to your financial well-being.

Firstly, identify the key destinations for your money. These may include your savings account, your 401k, and any other investment or goal-specific accounts. Creating a mental map of where you want your money to go is the initial step towards building a structured and purposeful financial routine.

Now, armed with this clarity, leverage the tools at your disposal – your bank's online platform, financial apps, or employer's direct deposit system. Log in to your accounts and navigate to the section that allows for setting up automatic transfers. This might be labeled as "Transfer," "Auto-Pay," or "Scheduled Payments" depending on the platform.

Once you've located the right section, the system will prompt you to input details such as the destination account, transfer amount, and frequency. This is where the beauty of automation truly shines – you have the flexibility to tailor these parameters to match your financial goals and paycheck schedule.

Consider the 401k as a priority destination for a portion of your paycheck. Setting up automatic contributions to your 401k ensures that you consistently invest in your future without the need for manual intervention. Many employers offer a direct deposit option for 401k contributions, making the process seamless and efficient.

Simultaneously, allocate a designated percentage or fixed amount to be transferred to your savings account. This ensures that a portion of your income is consistently set aside for emergencies, goals, or unforeseen expenses. Building this financial buffer becomes a cornerstone of your financial stability.

Keep in mind the importance of synchronization. If your payday varies or you receive income irregularly, align the automatic transfers with your specific schedule. This strategic synchronization ensures that your financial routine adapts to the cadence of your income, creating a harmonious and sustainable system.

A pro-tip is to set up these transfers shortly after your paycheck hits your account. This immediacy ensures that your financial goals are addressed promptly, leaving little room for the temptation to spend before saving or investing. Automating this process takes the burden off your shoulders, ensuring that your financial plan is executed consistently and without fail.

In conclusion, setting up automatic transfers is the hands-on component of the automation journey. It transforms the conceptual framework into tangible action, allowing your money to work for you effortlessly. By navigating your financial platform and configuring these transfers, you not only streamline your financial routine but also pave the way for a future where your financial goals are not just aspirations but concrete realities.

2.3 Connecting Your Paycheck to Your 401k

As we delve deeper into the intricacies of our three-step paycheck routine, a pivotal aspect emerges: connecting your paycheck to your 401k. This step is not just a financial maneuver; it's a strategic move towards securing your future and building a robust foundation for long-term wealth. Understanding how to navigate the landscape of 401k contributions is like unlocking a door to financial security, and it begins with the synergy between your paycheck and this powerful retirement investment account.

First and foremost, demystifying the 401k is essential. A 401k is a tax-advantaged retirement account offered by employers, allowing employees to contribute a portion of their pre-tax income toward investments. One of the primary advantages of a 401k is its potential for long-term growth, fueled by tax-deferred contributions and compounding interest. It's not just a retirement account; it's a vehicle for financial prosperity.

Now, let's explore the process of connecting your paycheck to your 401k. This often starts with your employer's human resources or benefits department. Many employers facilitate direct deposit into your 401k account, automating the contribution process right at the source – your paycheck. If this option is available, it's a seamless way to ensure a portion of your income is consistently allocated to your retirement savings without requiring manual transfers.

For those whose employers don't offer direct deposit into the 401k, fear not; there's still a straightforward approach. Once you've enrolled in your employer's 401k plan, you can set up automatic contributions through your online account. Navigate to the contribution or allocation section, and you'll likely find options to specify the percentage or fixed amount you want to contribute from each paycheck.

Deciding how much to contribute requires thoughtful consideration. While traditional advice often suggests aiming for 10-15% of your income, any contribution is a step in the right direction. If your financial circumstances are tight, start with a smaller percentage and gradually increase it as your income grows. The goal is to make consistent contributions that align with your financial goals without causing undue strain.

Timing is another critical factor. Aim to sync your 401k contributions with your payday. This synchronization ensures that the contribution occurs promptly after your paycheck hits your account, reducing the risk of spending before saving. Automating this connection between your paycheck and 401k contribution ensures that you're consistently building your retirement nest egg without the need for regular intervention.

The magic of connecting your paycheck to your 401k lies in the compound effect. As your contributions grow, so does the potential for investment returns. Over time, the compounding of contributions and returns can result in a substantial retirement fund. It's a strategy that leverages time, consistently contributing a portion of each paycheck to create a financial snowball that gains momentum as it rolls.

Understanding the impact of your 401k contributions extends beyond the present; it shapes your financial landscape in retirement. As contributions accumulate and investments grow, you're not merely saving; you're actively building a reservoir of financial security. It's a proactive approach that positions you to enjoy a more comfortable and fulfilling retirement, free from the financial anxieties that can accompany the later stages of life.

In conclusion, connecting your paycheck to your 401k is not just a transaction; it's a strategic decision that shapes the trajectory of your financial future. Whether through direct deposit or online contributions, this connection ensures that each paycheck propels you forward on the path to retirement readiness. It's an investment in your future self, illustrating the profound impact that small, consistent contributions can have on long-term financial well-being.

2.4 Allocating Funds to Your Savings and Investments

With the foundation of connecting your paycheck to your 401k laid, the next critical step in our three-step paycheck routine involves the strategic allocation of funds to your savings and investments. This step is not merely about setting money aside; it's about cultivating a financial ecosystem that nurtures your short-term goals and ensures a prosperous future. Understanding the art of allocating funds to your savings and investments is like crafting a masterpiece where each stroke contributes to the overall picture of financial success.

Begin by recognizing that your financial journey is multi-faceted. It comprises not only retirement planning but also short-term goals, emergencies, and opportunities. Allocating funds wisely involves creating a balanced approach that addresses both immediate needs and long-term aspirations.

One of the primary destinations for your paycheck allocations is your savings account. This serves as a financial safety net, shielding you from unexpected expenses or providing the means to seize spontaneous opportunities. Automating transfers to your savings account ensures a consistent buildup of this financial buffer, transforming it into a reliable resource for life's uncertainties.

When it comes to setting the amount to allocate to your savings, consider adopting a percentage-based approach. Aim for at least 5-10% of your paycheck to be directed to savings. This ensures that you're not just saving what's left at the end of the month but actively prioritizing savings from the moment your paycheck hits your account.

Simultaneously, embrace the power of specific savings goals. Whether it's a vacation, an emergency fund, or a down payment on a home, delineate your savings into categories. This level of specificity not only provides clarity on your financial objectives but also makes the act of saving more purposeful and rewarding.

Beyond savings, allocating funds to your investments propels you toward long-term wealth accumulation. Apart from your 401k contributions, consider setting up automatic transfers to other investment accounts, such as a Roth IRA or a brokerage account. Diversifying your investments ensures a robust portfolio that can weather market fluctuations and work toward your financial goals.

Setting the right allocation percentages for investments depends on your risk tolerance, financial goals, and timeline. If you're just starting, focus on a manageable percentage and gradually increase it as your financial situation evolves. The key is to establish consistency in your contributions, allowing time and compounding to work their magic.

Automation plays a pivotal role in this process. By configuring automatic transfers to your savings and investment accounts, you eliminate the need for constant decision-making. Your financial plan unfolds seamlessly, with each paycheck contributing to both your short-term stability and long-term growth.

Consider the psychological impact of this allocation strategy. By automating the process, you remove the stress associated with manual money management. Your funds are purposefully directed, creating a sense of financial order that permeates every aspect of your life. It's not just about building wealth; it's about fostering a mindset of financial control and empowerment.

As you navigate the allocation of funds, periodically revisit and reassess your goals. Life is dynamic, and your financial aspirations may evolve. Adjusting your allocations accordingly ensures that your paycheck routine remains aligned with your ever-changing financial landscape.

In conclusion, allocating funds to your savings and investments is the cornerstone of financial growth and stability. It's a conscious decision to prioritize both your present and future financial well-being. Through strategic automation and thoughtful goal-setting, you're not just managing money; you're sculpting a financial masterpiece that reflects your aspirations and paves the way for a prosperous tomorrow.

2.5 Troubleshooting and Pro Tips

Embarking on the journey of automating your money flow is a transformative endeavor, but like any significant change, it may encounter roadblocks. In this segment of our three-step paycheck routine, we delve into troubleshooting common issues and offer pro tips to enhance the efficiency of your automated financial system. Navigating potential challenges with finesse ensures that your financial journey remains on course, empowering you to overcome hurdles and emerge stronger on the path to financial well-being.

Troubleshooting Common Issues:

Irregular Income:

Challenge: What if your income doesn't adhere to a regular schedule?

Solution: Tailor the automated system to match your unique paycheck schedule. You can either replicate the system on the first and fifteenth of the month with half the money each time or maintain a buffer to simulate a monthly income schedule.

Unexpected Expenses:

Challenge: How to handle unexpected expenses that disrupt the automated flow?

Solution: Use the buffer in your checking account to cover unforeseen costs. Adjust the buffer amount based on your average monthly expenses to ensure stability during unexpected financial twists.

Automation Glitches:

Challenge: What if automated transfers fail or encounter glitches?

Solution: Leave a buffer amount in your checking account initially. Monitor the first few months to ensure seamless transactions. If an issue arises, contact your financial institution promptly. Use a prepared script to request fee waivers for any overdraft charges incurred due to technical glitches.

Pro Tips for Optimal Automation:

Sync Transfers with Payday:

Schedule automatic transfers to coincide with your payday. This immediate allocation minimizes the temptation to spend before saving or investing. Synchronization ensures a seamless and timely execution of your financial plan.

Percentage-Based Allocations:

Adopt a percentage-based approach when allocating funds to savings and investments. Aim for at least 5-10% directed to savings and set a manageable percentage for investments. Gradually increase these percentages as your financial situation evolves.

Specific Savings Goals:

Delineate your savings into specific goals, such as emergency funds, vacations, or major purchases. This not only adds purpose to your savings but also provides clarity on your financial objectives.

Regularly Reassess Goals:

Periodically revisit and reassess your financial goals. Life is dynamic, and your aspirations may evolve. Adjust your allocations accordingly to ensure that your automated system aligns with your ever-changing financial landscape.

Utilize Technology:

Leverage financial apps and online platforms to streamline the automation process. Many banking institutions offer user-friendly interfaces for setting up automatic transfers. Embrace technology to make financial management a seamless and convenient experience.

Maintain a Financial Safety Net:

Preserve a buffer amount in your checking account, especially during the initial setup. This safety net provides leeway in case of delayed paychecks or unforeseen glitches, offering a protective barrier against potential financial disruptions.

Regularly Review Statements:

Stay actively engaged with your finances by regularly reviewing statements. Set up email notifications for bill reminders and statements. This not only enhances your sense of control but also keeps you informed about your financial transactions.

In conclusion, troubleshooting and pro tips serve as the compass guiding you through the complexities of automating your money flow. As you encounter challenges, view them as opportunities for refinement and improvement. With the right strategies and proactive measures, your automated financial system becomes a robust and reliable ally on your journey to a financially secure and prosperous future.

Chapter 3: Step Two - Fine-Tuning Your Automatic Money Flow

3.1 Setting Payment Dates Strategically

As we delve into the intricacies of our three-step paycheck routine, Step Two emerges as the art of fine-tuning your automatic money flow. Beyond the initial setup, this step focuses on the strategic orchestration of payment dates – a nuanced approach that transforms your financial routine from functional to optimal. In this chapter, we explore the significance of setting payment dates strategically and how this seemingly small detail can yield substantial benefits in your journey toward financial mastery.

Understanding the Importance of Payment Date Strategy:

The timing of financial transactions holds more influence than meets the eye. Imagine a symphony where each instrument plays its part in harmony; similarly, setting payment dates strategically orchestrates a financial symphony that resonates with precision. This deliberate approach is not about arbitrary dates but aligning your financial commitments with the rhythm of your income.

Aligning with Paydays:

Consider synchronizing your payment dates with your payday. This alignment ensures that crucial financial commitments, such as bills and savings transfers, occur promptly after your paycheck lands in your account. By strategically linking these events, you minimize the risk of spending impulsively before addressing essential financial responsibilities.

Consolidating Payment Dates:

Aim for consolidation when selecting payment dates. Having multiple due dates scattered throughout the month can lead to a fragmented and chaotic financial experience. Consolidation streamlines your financial management, creating a focused window where you address bills and allocations in a structured manner.

Accounting for Processing Time:

Recognize the processing time required for different financial transactions. Whether it's automatic transfers, bill payments, or credit card settlements, accounting for processing time ensures that your financial commitments are met without the stress of last-minute rushes or potential late fees.

Strategic Steps to Set Payment Dates:

Review Current Billing Cycles:

Begin by reviewing your existing billing cycles. Identify due dates for bills, loan payments, and other recurring financial obligations. This comprehensive overview serves as the canvas upon which you'll strategically paint your payment schedule.

Contact Service Providers:

Proactively engage with service providers, creditors, and financial institutions. Many offer flexibility in adjusting billing cycles or due dates. Leverage this flexibility to tailor your payment dates in a way that complements your income schedule.

Utilize Online Platforms:

Leverage the capabilities of online banking platforms and financial apps. Most platforms allow users to customize payment dates for recurring transactions. Explore these settings to fine-tune your payment schedule with precision.

Consider Due Date Alignment:

Aim to align due dates with your payday or a specific window following your payday. This alignment creates a streamlined flow where your financial commitments are met with the influx of your paycheck, promoting financial stability.

Factor in Buffer Days:

Incorporate buffer days when setting payment dates. This cushion accounts for unexpected delays in paycheck processing or unforeseen circumstances, providing a safety net against potential financial disruptions.

The Art of Financial Symphony:

Setting payment dates strategically is akin to conducting a financial symphony where every note is played with purpose and timing is of the essence. It transforms the mundane task of bill payments into a choreography of financial mastery, where your income and obligations dance in harmony.

By fine-tuning your automatic money flow through strategic payment date selection, you not only optimize your financial routine but also cultivate a sense of control and confidence in your financial decisions. As you navigate Step Two of our three-step paycheck routine, envision your financial life as a symphony, and let the strategic setting of payment dates compose the melodious rhythm of your journey toward lasting financial well-being.

3.2 Transitioning to a Single Billing Date

In the orchestration of your financial symphony, the transition to a single billing date emerges as a harmonious strategy that elevates your financial routine to new heights of efficiency and clarity. This deliberate shift from scattered due dates to a unified billing calendar holds transformative power, streamlining your financial responsibilities and instilling a sense of control. In this chapter, we explore the nuances of transitioning to a single billing date and unravel the benefits that accompany this strategic move.

The Pervasive Challenge of Scattered Due Dates:

The conventional approach to managing bills often involves a scattered array of due dates spread across the calendar. Rent or mortgage payments, utility bills, credit card dues – each with its designated day of reckoning. This scattered landscape can lead to mental clutter, financial stress, and the constant juggling of due dates, detracting from the smooth rhythm of your financial symphony.

Benefits of a Single Billing Date:

Clarity and Simplicity:

Transitioning to a single billing date injects a dose of clarity into your financial landscape. No longer do you need to track multiple due dates; instead, you operate on a singular rhythm, simplifying your financial routine and reducing mental clutter.

Ease of Budgeting:

With a unified billing calendar, budgeting becomes a more straightforward endeavor. You can allocate funds with precision, knowing that a specific date marks the convergence of your financial commitments. This clarity enhances your ability to plan and manage your finances effectively.

Reduced Administrative Burden:

Managing bills becomes a streamlined administrative task with a single billing date. The need to monitor and schedule payments across various dates diminishes, freeing up mental bandwidth for more strategic financial considerations.

Enhanced Cash Flow Management:

A unified billing date contributes to improved cash flow management. Knowing when a significant portion of your financial obligations is due allows for better anticipation and allocation of funds. This proactive approach minimizes the risk of unexpected financial strains.

Strategic Steps to Transition:

Audit Existing Due Dates:

Begin the transition by conducting a comprehensive audit of your existing due dates. Identify all recurring bills, loan payments, and financial obligations, noting their respective due dates. This audit serves as the foundation for the strategic transition.

Engage with Service Providers:

Proactively engage with your service providers and creditors. Many companies offer flexibility in adjusting billing cycles or due dates. Initiate a conversation to explore options for aligning your billing dates.

Prioritize Transition:

Prioritize the transition to a single billing date in stages. Begin with bills that offer greater flexibility or those with providers open to adjusting due dates. Gradually work towards aligning all significant financial obligations on a single, strategic date.

Utilize Online Banking Tools:

Leverage the capabilities of online banking tools and financial apps. Many platforms allow users to customize due dates for recurring transactions. Explore these settings to facilitate the transition and ensure a smooth consolidation of billing dates.

Communicate Changes:

Communicate any changes in billing dates proactively. Notify your financial institutions and service providers about the transition to a unified billing calendar. This ensures a seamless transition and reduces the risk of oversights or misunderstandings.

Embracing Financial Harmony:

The transition to a single billing date is more than a mere administrative shift; it's a deliberate step towards financial harmony. As you consolidate due dates and streamline your financial obligations, envision a symphony where each note resonates on a chosen date, contributing to the melodious rhythm of your financial journey.

In conclusion, transitioning to a single billing date is a strategic move that transcends the mundanity of due dates. It's a conscious decision to align your financial responsibilities with precision and simplicity. As you navigate this transition in Step Two of our three-step paycheck routine, embrace the enhanced clarity and efficiency that accompanies a unified billing calendar – a key element in composing the symphony of financial mastery.

3.3 Automating Bill Payments and Credit Card Balances

As we continue our exploration into Step Two of the three-step paycheck routine, the spotlight now turns to the pivotal aspect of automating bill payments and credit card balances. This strategic maneuver is akin to fine-tuning the instruments in a financial symphony, ensuring that each note resonates seamlessly and contributes to the harmonious rhythm of your financial routine. In this chapter, we unravel the significance of automating these critical elements, unlocking a realm of convenience, reliability, and financial control.

The Essence of Automation:

At the heart of financial mastery lies the art of automation. It transcends the conventional method of manually managing bill payments and credit card balances, replacing it with a systematic and efficient approach. Automation is the conductor that orchestrates your financial symphony, allowing you to sit back and enjoy the melody of a well-organized financial routine.

Benefits of Automated Bill Payments:

Timely Payments:

Automation ensures that your bills are paid promptly and consistently. By linking your checking account to bill payments, you eliminate the risk of overlooking due dates or experiencing delays. Timely payments contribute to a positive credit history and shield you from unnecessary late fees.

Reduced Administrative Load:

Manually managing multiple bills can be an administrative burden. Automation streamlines this process, freeing you from the tedious task of individually scheduling payments. With a set-it-and-forget-it approach, you can redirect your focus to more strategic aspects of financial planning.

Avoidance of Late Fees:

Late fees can be a significant financial strain. Automating bill payments acts as a safeguard against late fees by ensuring that funds are allocated to cover obligations on time. This proactive approach shields your budget from unexpected financial setbacks.

Enhanced Credit Scor

Consistent, on-time bill payments positively impact your credit score. Automation becomes a powerful ally in maintaining a stellar credit history, opening doors to favorable financial opportunities in the future.

Strategic Steps to Automate:

Compile a List of Bills:

Begin by compiling a comprehensive list of all your recurring bills. Include utilities, rent or mortgage payments, subscription services, and any other financial obligations with regular due dates.

Utilize Online Bill Pay Features:

Leverage the online bill pay features offered by your banking institution. Most banks provide a user-friendly interface where you can set up automatic bill payments. Explore these features and customize the payment dates for each bill.

Coordinate Credit Card Payments:

Extend automation to your credit card balances. Link your credit card to your checking account and set up automatic payments for the statement balance. This ensures that your credit card is paid in full each month, preventing the accrual of high-interest charges.

Review Statements Regularly:

While automation brings convenience, it's essential to remain vigilant. Regularly review your statements to verify that automatic payments align with your expectations. This habit ensures that you stay informed about your financial transactions.

Set Up Email Notifications:

Enable email notifications for bill reminders and credit card statements. This proactive approach keeps you informed and provides an additional layer of control over your financial obligations.

Embracing Financial Freedom:

Automating bill payments and credit card balances is not just a technological convenience; it's a strategic move towards financial freedom. By relinquishing the manual burden of managing these elements, you empower yourself to focus on broader financial goals and aspirations.

As you navigate through the automated landscape of Step Two, envision a financial symphony where bill payments and credit card balances seamlessly integrate into the orchestrated rhythm of your financial routine. Embrace the convenience, reliability, and control that automation brings, propelling you toward a future of financial mastery and well-being.

3.4 Simplifying Your Financial Life with Automation

In the intricate dance of managing personal finances, simplicity is often the unsung hero. Step Two of our three-step paycheck routine introduces a transformative concept – simplifying your financial life with automation. This chapter delves into the art of streamlining complexities, reducing mental clutter, and embracing a financial routine that operates seamlessly. As we explore the realm of simplicity through automation, envision a harmonious financial symphony where each element effortlessly falls into place.

The Beauty of Simplicity:

In a world saturated with financial intricacies, the pursuit of simplicity emerges as a revolutionary concept. Simplifying your financial life is not about sacrificing control; instead, it's a deliberate choice to enhance control by reducing unnecessary complexities. Automation becomes the brushstroke that paints simplicity across your financial canvas.

Benefits of Simplifying with Automation:

Reduced Cognitive Load:

Juggling multiple due dates, transactions, and financial obligations can impose a significant cognitive load. Automation alleviates this burden by handling routine tasks, allowing you to redirect mental energy towards strategic financial decisions.

Enhanced Focus on Goals:

A simplified financial life grants you the mental bandwidth to focus on broader financial goals. Whether it's saving for a dream vacation, building an emergency fund, or investing for the future, automation becomes the enabler that frees you from the minutiae of day-to-day financial management.

Mitigation of Human Error:

Human error is an inherent risk in manual financial processes. Automation acts as a safeguard against oversight, miscalculations, or forgetfulness. By entrusting routine tasks to automated systems, you minimize the risk of financial missteps.

Consistent Financial Behavior:

Consistency is the hallmark of financial success. Automation ensures that your financial behavior remains consistent over time. Bills are paid on schedule, savings contributions are automated, and investments occur systematically – fostering a disciplined approach to financial management.

Strategic Steps to Simplify through Automation:

Consolidate Accounts:

Consider consolidating your financial accounts. Streamlining accounts reduces the complexity of managing multiple institutions and logins. A consolidated approach enhances visibility and facilitates a more straightforward overview of your financial landscape.

Utilize Financial Apps:

Explore financial apps that offer comprehensive automation features. Many apps provide functionalities for budgeting, bill payments, and investment tracking. Select an app that aligns with your financial goals and integrates seamlessly with your existing accounts.

Implement the 50/30/20 Rule:

Embrace the 50/30/20 rule for budgeting – 50% for needs, 30% for wants, and 20% for savings and investments. Automation becomes particularly impactful when adhering to this rule, ensuring that each paycheck is allocated to these categories without manual intervention.

Regularly Review and Adjust:

While automation brings simplicity, it's essential to maintain an active role in your financial management. Regularly review automated transactions, assess your financial goals, and make adjustments as needed. This proactive approach ensures that automation aligns with your evolving financial landscape.

Educate Yourself on Automated Tools:

Invest time in understanding the capabilities of automated tools. Whether it's online banking features, budgeting apps, or investment platforms, a comprehensive understanding empowers you to leverage automation effectively.

Embracing a Simpler Tomorrow:

Simplifying your financial life with automation is not a compromise; it's a strategic decision to unlock a future characterized by clarity, consistency, and control. As you navigate Step Two of our three-step paycheck routine, envision a financial landscape where complexity is replaced by simplicity – a terrain where automation becomes the guiding force in your journey towards lasting financial well-being.

In conclusion, the art of simplifying through automation transcends mere convenience; it's a profound shift towards a financial existence marked by ease and focus. Embrace the beauty of simplicity as automation weaves its thread through the fabric of your financial routine, transforming it into a masterpiece of efficiency and tranquility.

Chapter 4: Step Three - Tweaking the System to Fit Your Schedule

4.1 Adapting for Irregular Income

In the grand symphony of personal finance, adapting the melodic strains of a paycheck routine to the cadence of irregular income marks the crescendo of financial mastery. Step Three of our three-step paycheck routine invites you to embrace the art of tweaking the system to fit your unique schedule, especially if the rhythm of your income resembles more of a jazz improvisation than a classical composition. In this chapter, we explore the nuances of adapting for irregular income, orchestrating a harmonious financial routine that resonates with the unpredictability of life.

Understanding Irregular Income:

Irregular income is a common refrain for freelancers, entrepreneurs, and those engaged in the gig economy. The ebb and flow of earnings can be both exhilarating and challenging, demanding a tailored approach to financial management. Unlike the predictable cadence of a monthly salary, irregular income requires a delicate dance of flexibility and foresight.

Strategic Steps for Adapting:

Build a Buffer:

The cornerstone of adapting to irregular income lies in constructing a robust financial buffer. This buffer acts as a safety net during lean months, providing the necessary cushion to cover essential expenses when income fluctuates. Aim for a buffer that equals three to six months' worth of living expenses.

Diversify Income Streams:

Embrace the concept of diversification by cultivating multiple income streams. This strategic approach mitigates the impact of income volatility, ensuring a more consistent flow of funds. Explore opportunities for side gigs, freelance work, or passive income streams to augment your financial resilience.

Adjust Payment Dates:

Tailor your financial routine by adjusting payment dates to align with the influx of irregular income. If a significant payment is due shortly after a period of high earnings, consider shifting the due date to a more financially opportune time. Communication with service providers can often yield flexibility in this regard.

Utilize Variable Savings Contributions:

Introduce variability into your savings contributions. Rather than adhering to a fixed percentage, allocate a flexible portion of your irregular income to savings. During lucrative months, channel a higher percentage towards savings to fortify your financial foundation.

Periodic Financial Check-Ins:

Irregular income demands vigilant monitoring. Schedule periodic financial check-ins to assess your cash flow, review upcoming expenses, and make proactive adjustments. This regular evaluation ensures that your financial ship remains steady, even in the face of income variability.

Embracing the Dance of Irregularity:

Adapting for irregular income is not a meticulous choreography but a dynamic dance that responds to the rhythm of life's unpredictability. As you navigate the intricate steps of Step Three, envision a financial routine that seamlessly accommodates the irregularities of your income, transforming them into opportunities for financial resilience and growth.

Case Study: The Freelancer's Symphony

Consider a freelancer who experiences months of abundance followed by a quieter period. During the prosperous months, they allocate a higher percentage to savings and investments, fortifying their financial position. When income dwindles, the buffer they meticulously built becomes the financial lifeline, ensuring stability during the quieter interludes. This adaptive approach transforms irregularity from a challenge into a strategic element of their financial symphony.

In conclusion, adapting for irregular income is a personalized journey that invites you to become the conductor of your financial orchestra. By building buffers, diversifying income, and adjusting your financial routine, you transform irregularity from a source of stress into a dynamic element that enriches your financial narrative. As you traverse the landscape of Step Three, envision a financial routine that mirrors the fluidity of your income, creating a symphony where every note contributes to the harmonious melody of financial well-being.

4.2 Option One: Bi-Monthly Paycheck Replication

In the intricate dance of financial planning, adapting a paycheck routine to the nuances of irregular income requires a tailored approach. Option One presents a compelling strategy – the replication of a bi-monthly paycheck system. This method, akin to choreographing a financial pas de deux, enables individuals with irregular income to synchronize their financial routine with the cadence of their earnings. In this exploration of Option One, we unravel the intricacies of bi-monthly paycheck replication and its transformative impact on financial stability.

Understanding Bi-Monthly Paycheck Replication:

For individuals grappling with irregular income, the conventional monthly paycheck routine may seem ill-suited to their financial reality. Option One introduces a novel concept – replicating the structure of a bi-monthly paycheck system. Instead of waiting for a singular monthly influx of funds, this approach divides income into two distinct periods, mimicking the rhythm of a semi-monthly salary. This deliberate division allows for a more strategic allocation of resources and the creation of financial checkpoints.

Strategic Steps for Implementation:

Income Division:

Begin by dividing your irregular income into two portions, aligning with a bi-monthly schedule. This division sets the stage for a more structured financial routine, providing clarity and predictability amid the irregularities of earnings.

Expense Alignment:

Sync your major expenses with the two income periods. Strategically allocate bills, rent, and significant financial obligations to coincide with the bi-monthly influx of funds. This synchronization minimizes the risk of financial strain during leaner periods.

Savings and Investments:

Allocate a specific percentage of each bi-monthly income segment to savings and investments. This disciplined approach ensures a consistent focus on building financial reserves and nurturing long-term wealth. Dedicating a portion of each paycheck to these goals becomes a non-negotiable aspect of the financial routine.

Buffer Maintenance:

Emphasize the importance of maintaining a financial buffer. Irregular income inherently involves fluctuations, and a robust buffer acts as a financial safety net. Allocate a portion of each paycheck replication cycle to fortify this buffer, providing resilience during low-income phases.

Periodic Review and Adjustment:

Schedule regular reviews of your financial plan to assess its effectiveness. Adaptations may be necessary based on changes in income patterns or unexpected financial shifts. This periodic evaluation ensures that the bi-monthly replication remains finely tuned to your unique financial circumstances.

Case Study: The Bi-Monthly Ballet

Consider a freelancer who embraces the bi-monthly paycheck replication strategy. During months of heightened earnings, they diligently allocate funds to cover essential expenses, savings, and investments for the first half of the month. As the second income segment arrives, they strategically address additional expenses, fine-tune savings contributions, and assess the overall financial landscape. This rhythmic approach transforms irregularity into a choreographed financial ballet.

Benefits of Option One:

Enhanced Financial Predictability:

The bi-monthly replication injects a dose of predictability into the irregular income scenario. By segmenting income and expenses, individuals gain a clearer understanding of their financial rhythm, reducing uncertainty.

Strategic Resource Allocation:

Resources are allocated strategically across the bi-monthly cycles, ensuring that essential needs, savings, and investments receive consistent attention. This intentional distribution enhances financial stability and fosters a disciplined approach to money management.

Mitigation of High-Low Income Disparities:

Irregular income often entails fluctuations between high and low-earning periods. The bi-monthly replication helps mitigate the impact of these disparities by providing a structured framework for financial decision-making.

Buffer Reinforcement:

The deliberate allocation of funds to a financial buffer during each cycle reinforces resilience. This buffer serves as a financial lifeline during leaner periods, offering peace of mind and stability.

Embracing Financial Ballet:

Option One, the bi-monthly paycheck replication, unfolds as a financial ballet where income and expenses gracefully waltz in synchrony. This approach transforms irregularity into a choreographed routine, empowering individuals to navigate the complexities of their financial landscape with poise and precision. As you consider this option within Step Three of the three-step paycheck routine, envision a financial ballet where each pirouette represents a deliberate step toward financial well-being.

4.3 Option Two: Creating and Using a Savings Buffer

In the realm of adapting financial strategies to irregular income, Option Two emerges as a pragmatic and resilient approach – the creation and utilization of a savings buffer. For individuals whose income resembles more of a fluctuating symphony than a steady beat, this option offers a strategic response to the unpredictability of earnings. In this exploration, we delve into the intricacies of Option Two, unveiling the art of building and deploying a savings buffer to navigate the undulating landscape of irregular income.

Understanding the Savings Buffer Concept:

A savings buffer serves as a financial cushion, a reserve strategically designed to weather the highs and lows of irregular income. Unlike traditional emergency funds, which cater primarily to unforeseen expenses, a savings buffer for irregular income caters specifically to fluctuations in earnings. It acts as a proactive tool, enabling individuals to maintain financial stability during periods of lower income while capitalizing on opportunities during prosperous phases.

Strategic Steps for Implementation:

Determining Buffer Size:

Begin by assessing your monthly living expenses. Calculate the sum of essential costs such as rent, utilities, groceries, and loan payments. Aim to create a buffer that covers three to six months' worth of these fundamental expenses. This calculated approach ensures that the buffer aligns with your specific financial needs.

Building the Buffer:

Systematically contribute a portion of each income influx to the savings buffer. Treat this contribution as a non-negotiable aspect of your financial routine, emphasizing consistency. During months of elevated income, allocate a higher percentage to expedite buffer growth.

Deploying During Low-Income Periods:

The savings buffer serves as a dynamic resource during periods of reduced income. When earnings dip, strategically deploy funds from the buffer to cover essential expenses. This deliberate utilization mitigates financial strain, offering a sense of security during leaner phases.

Replenishing During High-Income Periods:

During months of heightened earnings, focus on replenishing the savings buffer. Allocate a percentage of surplus income to fortify the buffer, ensuring its resilience for future use. This cyclical process transforms the savings buffer into a sustainable financial safety net.

Continuous Monitoring and Adjustment:

Regularly monitor the health of your savings buffer and make adjustments as needed. Factors such as changes in income patterns, unexpected expenses, or shifts in financial goals may necessitate alterations to the buffer size or contribution percentages. Adaptability is key to optimizing the effectiveness of the savings buffer.

Case Study: The Savings Symphony

Imagine an individual navigating the gig economy, experiencing variable income streams. They diligently implement Option Two by building a savings buffer tailored to cover three months of essential expenses. During months of lower income, they seamlessly draw from the buffer to maintain financial stability. As income surges, they prioritize replenishing the buffer, ensuring its continuous efficacy. This strategic dance transforms the irregular income symphony into a harmonious savings symphony.

Benefits of Option Two:

Financial Resilience:

The savings buffer acts as a shield against income volatility, providing financial resilience during periods of reduced earnings. This resilience enhances the ability to navigate financial challenges with confidence.

Strategic Resource Allocation:

The deliberate deployment of the savings buffer strategically allocates resources during low-income phases. This ensures that essential expenses are covered, minimizing financial strain and fostering stability.

Opportunistic Capitalization:

During high-income periods, the savings buffer becomes a resource for opportunistic capitalization. Individuals can channel surplus funds into long-term goals, investments, or strategic financial moves, leveraging the buffer for financial growth.

Adaptability to Fluctuations:

The savings buffer adapts to the ebb and flow of irregular income. Its dynamic nature allows for continuous adjustments, aligning with changes in income patterns or financial objectives.

Navigating the Symphony of Irregular Income:

Option Two, the creation and utilization of a savings buffer, unfolds as a financial symphony where adaptability and strategic planning harmonize. This approach transforms irregularity into an orchestrated routine, providing individuals with the tools to navigate the undulating financial landscape with grace and resilience. As you explore this option within Step Three of the three-step paycheck routine, envision a savings symphony where each note contributes to the melody of financial well-being.

4.4 Building Stability with a 3-Month Savings Goal

Amidst the dynamic landscape of irregular income, Option Three emerges as a beacon of stability – the establishment and pursuit of a 3-month savings goal. This strategic approach acknowledges the fluctuating nature of earnings while fostering financial resilience through the targeted accumulation of savings. In this exploration, we delve into the intricacies of Option Three, unraveling the art of building stability by setting and achieving a 3-month savings goal.

Setting the Foundation:

Recognizing that irregular income demands a unique financial approach, Option Three centers on the creation of a savings goal tailored to cover three months of living expenses. This goal serves as a tangible anchor, providing individuals with a concrete target to strive for in the quest for financial stability. The deliberate pursuit of this goal transforms the unpredictable into the manageable, fostering a sense of control over one's financial narrative.

Strategic Steps for Implementation:

Calculate Essential Living Expenses:

Begin by meticulously calculating your essential living expenses. This encompasses rent or mortgage payments, utilities, groceries, loan payments, and any other non-negotiable costs required for day-to-day living. This comprehensive assessment forms the foundation for determining the target savings amount.

Define the 3-Month Savings Goal:

Set a savings goal equivalent to three months' worth of essential living expenses. This goal establishes a financial threshold that, once achieved, provides a robust safety net during leaner months. The specificity of a 3-month horizon enhances clarity and motivation in the pursuit of stability.

Consistent Contribution Strategy:

Develop a consistent contribution strategy towards your 3-month savings goal. Allocate a percentage of each income influx exclusively to this goal, treating it as a priority within your financial routine. Consistency in contributions accelerates progress and instills discipline in your financial habits.

Periodic Goal Assessment:

Periodically assess your progress toward the 3-month savings goal. Regular check-ins allow for adjustments based on changes in income patterns, unexpected expenses, or shifts in financial priorities. This adaptive approach ensures that the savings goal remains both realistic and aligned with your evolving circumstances.

Celebrating Milestones:

Break down the pursuit of the 3-month savings goal into manageable milestones. Celebrate each achievement, whether it be completing one month's worth of savings or reaching the halfway point. Milestone celebrations serve as motivational checkpoints, reinforcing the positive impact of your financial efforts.

Case Study: The Pursuit of Stability

Consider an individual navigating the irregular income terrain, grappling with the ebb and flow of earnings. Embracing Option Three, they set a 3-month savings goal tailored to cover essential living expenses. With a consistent contribution strategy, they diligently allocate a percentage of each income influx toward this goal. As milestones are achieved, a sense of stability emerges, transforming the pursuit into a tangible reality.

Benefits of Option Three:

Tangible Financial Anchor:

The 3-month savings goal acts as a tangible anchor, providing a clear and measurable target. This specificity enhances motivation and instills a sense of purpose in the pursuit of financial stability.

Strategic Allocation of Resources:

The consistent contribution strategy ensures a strategic allocation of resources toward the savings goal. This focused approach accelerates progress and reinforces disciplined financial habits.

Adaptability to Changing Circumstances:

Periodic goal assessments allow for adaptability to changing circumstances. Whether facing fluctuations in income or unexpected expenses, the ability to recalibrate the savings goal ensures its continued relevance and achievability.

Milestone Motivation:

Breaking down the pursuit into milestones introduces a motivational element. Celebrating achievements along the way fosters a positive financial mindset and reinforces the impact of intentional savings.

Embracing Stability in Irregularity:

Option Three, building stability with a 3-month savings goal, unfolds as a journey towards financial resilience and predictability. This approach transforms the inherent irregularity of income into a structured pursuit, where stability becomes an achievable reality. As you explore this option within Step Three of the three-step paycheck routine, envision a path where each step toward the 3-month savings goal echoes the pursuit of financial stability in the midst of irregularity.

Chapter 5: Achieving Financial Mastery

5.1 Embracing the Rich Life

In the culmination of the three-step paycheck routine, achieving financial mastery transcends mere monetary management. It beckons individuals to not only navigate the intricacies of income and expenses but to embark on a holistic journey towards embracing the rich life. The concept of a rich life extends beyond financial abundance; it encapsulates the harmonious integration of wealth, purpose, and joy. As we delve into this final chapter, the emphasis shifts from monetary transactions to the profound exploration of what it means to truly live a rich and fulfilling life.

Embracing the Rich Life:

At its core, the rich life is not a destination but a dynamic and evolving state of being. It is about crafting a life that aligns with one's values, aspirations, and personal definitions of fulfillment. Financial mastery becomes a means to an end, facilitating the pursuit of experiences, relationships, and contributions that enrich the tapestry of one's existence. The journey towards the rich life commences with a shift in mindset – a departure from the scarcity mentality towards an abundance mentality.

Key Components of the Rich Life:

Purposeful Spending:

Embracing the rich life involves a shift from mindless consumption to purposeful spending. Individuals are encouraged to allocate resources towards experiences, relationships, and endeavors that resonate with their passions and contribute to their overall well-being. The focus shifts from acquiring possessions to curating a life rich in meaning and significance.

Investing in Personal Growth:

Financial mastery becomes a catalyst for personal growth. The rich life encompasses a commitment to continuous learning, skill development, and self-discovery. Investing in education, whether formal or informal, becomes a pathway to expanding one's capabilities and unlocking new opportunities.

Contributions to Others:

A hallmark of the rich life is the recognition of one's ability to positively impact the lives of others. Financial resources, when harnessed purposefully, enable individuals to contribute to causes, charities, and initiatives that align with their values. The act of giving back becomes an integral part of the rich life journey.

Cultivating Healthy Relationships:

True wealth extends beyond monetary assets to encompass the richness of relationships. Financial mastery supports the cultivation of healthy connections with family, friends, and communities. The rich life thrives on the shared experiences, support systems, and meaningful connections that elevate the human experience.

Navigating the Transition:

Transitioning from financial management to embracing the rich life involves a mindful and intentional shift in priorities. It requires individuals to reassess their relationship with money, viewing it as a tool for empowerment rather than a source of stress. As financial goals are achieved and stability is established, the focus naturally expands beyond the constraints of budgeting and saving towards the expansive realm of possibilities that define the rich life.

Practical Strategies for Embracing the Rich Life:

Define Your Values:

Begin by clarifying your values and aspirations. What aspects of life bring you the greatest joy and fulfillment? Align your financial decisions with these values to ensure that your resources are directed towards what truly matters to you.

Create a Life Vision:

Envision the life you desire to lead. What experiences do you want to have? What contributions do you wish to make? Crafting a life vision provides a roadmap for financial decisions that align with your overarching goals.

Celebrate Milestones:

Celebrate not only financial milestones but also the milestones in your personal and experiential journey. Recognize and commemorate achievements, both big and small, fostering a sense of gratitude and accomplishment.

Practice Mindful Spending:

Shift towards mindful spending by evaluating the impact of purchases on your overall well-being. Consider whether a particular expenditure contributes to your rich life vision or detracts from it. Prioritize investments in experiences and relationships over material possessions.

The Ongoing Journey:

Achieving financial mastery and embracing the rich life is not a one-time accomplishment but an ongoing journey. It requires a commitment to self-reflection, adaptability to life's changes, and a continuous alignment of financial decisions with personal values. As individuals navigate this dynamic terrain, they find that the true wealth lies not just in the numbers on a balance sheet but in the richness of a life well-lived. The three-step paycheck routine serves as a foundation for this journey, offering a structured approach that empowers individuals to master their finances and unlock the full potential of the rich life.

5.2 Overcoming Common Challenges

In the pursuit of financial mastery and the realization of the rich life, individuals often encounter a myriad of challenges that can act as roadblocks on their journey. Acknowledging and overcoming these challenges becomes a crucial aspect of the transformative process, ensuring that the path to financial empowerment remains resilient and adaptable. In this exploration, we delve into some common challenges faced on the quest for financial mastery and provide strategies to navigate and conquer these hurdles.

Challenge 1: Unforeseen Expenses and Emergencies

Life is inherently unpredictable, and unexpected expenses or emergencies can pose a significant challenge to financial stability. Whether it's a sudden medical bill, car repair, or home maintenance, these unforeseen events can derail even the most carefully crafted financial plans.

Strategy: Establish an Emergency Fund

To mitigate the impact of unforeseen expenses, establish and consistently contribute to an emergency fund. This financial cushion serves as a buffer, providing a safety net to cover unexpected costs without jeopardizing your broader financial goals. Aim to accumulate three to six months' worth of living expenses in your emergency fund, ensuring you are prepared for unexpected twists on your financial journey.

Challenge 2: Temptation of Impulse Spending

In a world filled with enticing purchases and constant marketing messages, the temptation of impulse spending can undermine financial discipline. Succumbing to impulsive purchases can divert resources away from meaningful goals and contribute to a cycle of regret and frustration.

Strategy: Implement a Cooling-Off Period

Combat the allure of impulse spending by implementing a cooling-off period. Before making non-essential purchases, impose a waiting period, such as 24 hours or a week. This delay provides an opportunity to evaluate whether the purchase aligns with your values and financial priorities. Additionally, creating a budget and allocating specific funds for discretionary spending allows for guilt-free enjoyment without jeopardizing long-term financial objectives.

Challenge 3: Debt Accumulation

Accruing debt, whether through credit cards, loans, or other financial instruments, can hinder progress towards financial mastery. High-interest debt can quickly spiral out of control, leading to a cycle of repayments that diverts funds away from savings and investments.

Strategy: Prioritize Debt Repayment

Prioritize debt repayment as a fundamental component of your financial strategy. Develop a structured plan to tackle outstanding debts, focusing on high-interest obligations first. Consider consolidating debts or negotiating lower interest rates to accelerate the repayment process. As debts are gradually eliminated, redirect the freed-up funds towards savings and investments, reinforcing your journey towards financial empowerment.

Challenge 4: Lack of Financial Education

A lack of financial education can be a formidable obstacle on the path to financial mastery. Many individuals navigate complex financial landscapes without a comprehensive understanding of budgeting, investing, and long-term financial planning.

Strategy: Invest in Financial Education

Address the challenge of financial illiteracy by investing in ongoing financial education. Leverage resources such as books, online courses, and reputable financial websites to enhance your knowledge and skills. Consider seeking guidance from financial advisors or attending workshops that offer practical insights into effective money management. By continuously expanding your financial literacy, you empower yourself to make informed decisions and navigate the complexities of personal finance with confidence.

Challenge 5: External Pressures and Comparison

External pressures, coupled with the pervasive culture of comparison fueled by social media, can create a sense of inadequacy and hinder the pursuit of the rich life. Constant exposure to seemingly extravagant lifestyles can breed discontent and distract from one's unique financial journey.

Strategy: Define Your Own Metrics of Success

Counter the influence of external pressures by defining your own metrics of success. Recognize that the rich life is a deeply personal and subjective concept. Focus on your individual values, aspirations, and priorities rather than succumbing to external benchmarks. Regularly revisit and refine your financial goals based on your unique circumstances, ensuring that your journey towards financial mastery aligns authentically with your vision of the rich life.

The Resilient Path Forward:

Overcoming common challenges in the pursuit of financial mastery requires resilience, adaptability, and a commitment to continuous improvement. By proactively addressing unforeseen expenses, resisting impulse spending, prioritizing debt repayment, investing in financial education, and defining personal metrics of success, individuals can navigate these challenges with confidence. Embrace the challenges as opportunities for growth, recognizing that each hurdle conquered brings you closer to the financial mastery and rich life you aspire to achieve.

5.3 Long-Term Strategies for Financial Success

As individuals embark on the journey of financial mastery, adopting long-term strategies becomes pivotal in ensuring sustained success and enduring prosperity. Beyond the immediate tactics employed in daily money management, these overarching strategies lay the foundation for enduring financial well-being. In this exploration, we delve into the essential long-term strategies that contribute to a robust and resilient financial future.

Strategy 1: Cultivating Investment Mindset

A key pillar of long-term financial success is the cultivation of an investment mindset. Shifting focus from mere saving to strategic investing empowers individuals to make their money work for them. Embrace the principle of compound growth, wherein invested funds generate returns that, in turn, contribute to future growth. Whether through retirement accounts, index funds, or real estate, strategic investments form the bedrock of long-term financial prosperity.

Implementation: Diversified Portfolio and Consistent Contributions

Establish a diversified investment portfolio that aligns with your risk tolerance and financial goals. Spread investments across various asset classes to mitigate risk and enhance potential returns. Consistency in contributions, even in the face of market fluctuations, amplifies the impact of compounding over time. Regularly review and rebalance your portfolio to adapt to changing market conditions and ensure alignment with your long-term objectives.

Strategy 2: Prioritizing Financial Education and Adaptability

Long-term financial success necessitates an ongoing commitment to financial education and adaptability. The financial landscape evolves, presenting new opportunities and challenges. Individuals who prioritize continuous learning position themselves to navigate these changes with informed decision-making. Stay abreast of market trends, technological advancements, and legislative updates that may impact your financial strategy.

Implementation: Lifelong Learning and Adaptive Strategies

Engage in lifelong learning through books, courses, seminars, and reputable financial publications. Stay informed about advancements in financial technology that may offer innovative solutions for wealth management. Develop adaptive strategies that can flexibly respond to changes in income, expenses, and market conditions. By embracing a mindset of constant learning and adaptability, you equip yourself to thrive in an ever-evolving financial landscape.

Strategy 3: Building Robust Emergency and Retirement Funds

Long-term financial success is fortified by the establishment of robust emergency and retirement funds. These financial buffers act as pillars of stability, providing security during unforeseen crises and ensuring a comfortable retirement. Regular contributions to these funds exemplify a commitment to both short-term resilience and long-term security.

Implementation: Automated Contributions and Periodic Reviews

Automate contributions to your emergency and retirement funds to ensure consistency. Set clear goals for the size of these funds, taking into account living expenses, lifestyle preferences, and retirement aspirations. Periodically review and adjust these goals to reflect changing circumstances, such as career advancements, family changes, or shifts in economic conditions. By actively nurturing these financial safeguards, you pave the way for enduring financial stability.

Strategy 4: Establishing Legacy and Philanthropic Goals

A holistic approach to long-term financial success encompasses the establishment of legacy and philanthropic goals. Beyond personal wealth accumulation, consider the impact of your financial legacy on future generations and the community. Integrate philanthropy into your financial plan, aligning your resources with causes and initiatives that resonate with your values.

Implementation: Estate Planning and Charitable Giving

Engage in comprehensive estate planning to define the distribution of your assets in alignment with your legacy goals. Explore philanthropic endeavors and charitable giving strategies that reflect your values and contribute to positive societal impact. By considering the broader implications of your financial footprint, you contribute to a lasting legacy that extends beyond individual wealth.

Strategy 5: Foster Healthy Financial Habits

Sustainable financial success thrives on the foundation of healthy financial habits. Cultivate disciplined spending, conscientious budgeting, and proactive debt management. These habits not only contribute to short-term financial stability but also form the building blocks of a resilient and prosperous financial future.

Implementation: Consistent Budgeting and Debt Reduction

Adopt a consistent budgeting practice that aligns with your financial goals and priorities. Track and analyze spending patterns to identify areas for optimization. Prioritize debt reduction by developing a structured repayment plan, focusing on high-interest obligations first. By fostering healthy financial habits, you lay the groundwork for enduring financial success.

In navigating the long-term horizon of financial success, individuals are called upon to adopt a strategic and forward-thinking mindset. By cultivating an investment mindset, prioritizing financial education, building robust financial buffers, establishing legacy goals, and fostering healthy financial habits, individuals fortify their financial foundations. These enduring strategies, implemented with diligence and adaptability, empower individuals to traverse the complexities of the financial landscape with confidence and resilience. As the journey unfolds, the realization of long-term financial success becomes not merely an aspiration but a tangible and sustainable reality.

CONCLUSION

In conclusion, embracing the power of financial automation is not merely a pragmatic approach; it is a transformative journey toward empowerment and sustained financial well-being. Through the meticulous implementation of the three-step paycheck routine, individuals can revolutionize their relationship with money, transcending the constraints of traditional budgeting and achieving a richer, more fulfilling life.

The first crucial step involves the automation of money flow, directing funds with purpose and precision. By linking accounts, setting up automatic transfers, and connecting paychecks to essential financial vehicles like 401(k)s and savings accounts, individuals create a seamless and efficient system that operates effortlessly in the background.

The second step, fine-tuning the automatic money flow, is a strategic endeavor to set payment dates strategically and simplify financial obligations. By transitioning to a single billing date, automating bill payments, and balancing credit card balances, the financial landscape becomes clearer, more manageable, and less susceptible to oversights.

The third and final step is about adapting the system to fit individual schedules, whether dealing with irregular income or opting for bi-monthly paycheck replication. By building stability with a 3-month savings goal and strategically utilizing options like a savings buffer, individuals gain the flexibility to navigate the unpredictable nature of life without compromising their financial objectives.

In essence, this journey towards financial automation is a declaration of autonomy. It's a conscious decision to reclaim control over one's financial narrative, alleviate the burden of constant financial management, and redirect energy towards living a rich life. Through education, strategic planning, and a commitment to long-term financial success, individuals can truly empower themselves, transcending financial stress and embracing the abundance that comes with mastering the art of financial automation.

FREE 12 MONTH SAVING TRACKER

MONTH: # DAILY SAVINGS TRACKER

DATE	DESCRIPTION	DEPOSIT	WITHDRAWAL	BALANCE
		TOTAL		

MONTH:

DAILY SAVINGS
TRACKER

DATE	DESCRIPTION	DEPOSIT	WITHDRAWAL	BALANCE
	TOTAL			

MONTH:

DAILY SAVINGS
TRACKER

DATE	DESCRIPTION	DEPOSIT	WITHDRAWAL	BALANCE

TOTAL	

MONTH:

DAILY SAVINGS
TRACKER

DATE	DESCRIPTION	DEPOSIT	WITHDRAWAL	BALANCE
		TOTAL		

MONTH:

DAILY SAVINGS TRACKER

DATE	DESCRIPTION	DEPOSIT	WITHDRAWAL	BALANCE
		TOTAL		

MONTH:

DAILY SAVINGS
TRACKER

DATE	DESCRIPTION	DEPOSIT	WITHDRAWAL	BALANCE
		TOTAL		

MONTH: DAILY SAVINGS
TRACKER

DATE	DESCRIPTION	DEPOSIT	WITHDRAWAL	BALANCE
		TOTAL		

MONTH:

DAILY SAVINGS
TRACKER

DATE	DESCRIPTION	DEPOSIT	WITHDRAWAL	BALANCE
		TOTAL		

MONTH:

DAILY SAVINGS
TRACKER

DATE	DESCRIPTION	DEPOSIT	WITHDRAWAL	BALANCE
		TOTAL		

MONTH:

DAILY SAVINGS
TRACKER

DATE	DESCRIPTION	DEPOSIT	WITHDRAWAL	BALANCE
		TOTAL		

MONTH:

DAILY SAVINGS
TRACKER

DATE	DESCRIPTION	DEPOSIT	WITHDRAWAL	BALANCE
		TOTAL		

MONTH:

DAILY SAVINGS
TRACKER

DATE	DESCRIPTION	DEPOSIT	WITHDRAWAL	BALANCE
		TOTAL		

MONTH:

DAILY SAVINGS
TRACKER

DATE	DESCRIPTION	DEPOSIT	WITHDRAWAL	BALANCE
		TOTAL		

MONTH:

DAILY SAVINGS
TRACKER

DATE	DESCRIPTION	DEPOSIT	WITHDRAWAL	BALANCE
		TOTAL		

MONTH:

DAILY SAVINGS
TRACKER

DATE	DESCRIPTION	DEPOSIT	WITHDRAWAL	BALANCE
	TOTAL			

DAILY SAVINGS
TRACKER

DATE	DESCRIPTION	DEPOSIT	WITHDRAWAL	BALANCE
		TOTAL		

107

MONTH:

DAILY SAVINGS
TRACKER

DATE	DESCRIPTION	DEPOSIT	WITHDRAWAL	BALANCE
	TOTAL			

MONTH:

DAILY SAVINGS
TRACKER

DATE	DESCRIPTION	DEPOSIT	WITHDRAWAL	BALANCE
	TOTAL			

MONTH:

DAILY SAVINGS
TRACKER

DATE	DESCRIPTION	DEPOSIT	WITHDRAWAL	BALANCE
		TOTAL		

DAILY SAVINGS
TRACKER

DATE	DESCRIPTION	DEPOSIT	WITHDRAWAL	BALANCE
		TOTAL		

MONTH:

DAILY SAVINGS
TRACKER

DATE	DESCRIPTION	DEPOSIT	WITHDRAWAL	BALANCE

TOTAL	

DAILY SAVINGS TRACKER

DATE	DESCRIPTION	DEPOSIT	WITHDRAWAL	BALANCE
		TOTAL		

www.ingramcontent.com/pod-product-compliance
Lightning Source LLC
Chambersburg PA
CBHW071208290526
45796CB00008B/181